MW01232893

Take Charge of Your Financial Destiny

BY JERRY SAVELLE

Take Charge of Your Financial Destiny

ISBN 0-9655352-4-X

Unless otherwise stated, all scripture quotations are taken from The King James Version of the Bible.

Jerry Savelle Publications
P.O. Box 748
Crowley, TX 76036
817/297-3155

TABLE OF CONTENTS

Chapter 1

CHAPTER 1

You're Never Without Seed

Have you ever noticed that it seems just when you have extra money to do something you've been believing to do, suddenly all these unexpected needs arise? The electric bill is higher than usual – more money! The car needs repaired – more money! The kids need new clothes – more money! All these needs suddenly seem to come up out of nowhere and eventually consume all of your money. So what do you end up giving to God? Nothing. It was all consumed.

That's the way Satan operates. He knows when you have extra money in your possession so he creates all these little obstacles to leave you with nothing left for God.

There is something that you possess that Satan's after more than anything else in your life and that's seed. If he cannot get your seed, then he cannot defeat you. If he can get your seed, then he limits you.

When I first came to the Lord in 1969, my wife, Carolyn, and I were just two little kids from Shreveport, Louisiana, who knew we had the call of God on our lives. We had a lot of zeal. We were so excited about the things of God. We could hardly wait to get out in the middle of what God wanted us to do, but we didn't have anything to do it with. The car was shot. I didn't have a suit. I had uniforms that had "Jerry's Paint and Body Shop" written across the front. You can't preach in Jerry's Paint and Body Shop uniforms. But it didn't make any difference because there wasn't a church that wanted to hear me anyway.

God began to teach me in the very early stages of our Christianity that I may not always have what I need at the moment, but **I am never without the seed that will produce it.** You may not have everything you need right now, but I can promise you, you do have in your possession, at this very moment, the seed that will produce what you need.

> *Now he that ministereth seed to the sower both minister bread for your food, and multiply your seed sown, and increase the fruits of your righteousness.*
>
> 2 Corinthians 9:10

If there's one thing that God has provided for you and always will, it's seed. And if you learn to plant it properly, then He will multiply your seed sown, and He will also multiply your resources for sowing.

The most important thing which you possess that Satan is after is your seed. He wants your seed consumed before it can get into God's hands. He wants your seed devoured before you can give it to God. He wants you to spend all your seed. He wants you to waste all your seed. He wants you to throw away your seed. Why? Because seed is what makes you dangerous to him.

In this little book, you're going to learn how to protect your seed, sow it properly and keep it producing a maximum harvest. So keep reading, and get ready for a revelation that will change your life forever.

Chapter 2

CHAPTER 2

You Determine Your Own Destiny

The Lord asked me a question one time. He said, "When I created man, what was the first gift I bestowed upon him?" I said, "Genesis 1:26 says,

> *...let them have dominion over the fish of the sea, and over the fowl of the air, and over the cattle, and over all the earth, and over every creeping thing that creepeth upon the earth.*

The first gift was dominion and authority." He said, "That's right." Then He said, "What was the second gift I gave to man after creating him?" I had to be very honest because I had never thought of it in terms of gift number one and gift number two. So I said, "Lord, I don't know." He said, "Well, where did you find the first gift?" I said, "Genesis 1:26, 27, 28." He said, "Then if gift number one is in those verses, keep reading and you'll find gift number two." Verse 29 says,

And God said, Behold, I have given you every ***herb bearing seed.*** That . . . constitutes a gift.

In your Bible, there may be a footnote next to *herb bearing seed.* If you look in the center cross reference of your Bible, it will give you the original Hebrew rendering and it says: *seeding seed.*

> *I have given you every seeding seed which is upon the face of all the earth, and every tree, in the which is the fruit of a tree yielding seed; to you it shall be for meat.*
>
> Genesis 1:29

There are other translations that say *food or provision* instead of *meat.*

In other words, God said to Adam, "I'm going to give you two things, and with these two things you can determine your destiny: Number one - authority; number two - seed. With those two things no one can control you. No one can limit you. No one can restrict you. You determine your destiny through your God-given authority and by the seeds that you sow.

God has given you seed for provision. A lot of people have the idea that God did all the sowing and all the growing and Adam just walked around doing nothing. Why would He give him seed if it's not for sowing? Why do you call a place a garden if you don't plant something there?

Let's read what Adam was required to do in verse 15,

> *And the Lord God took the man, and put him into the garden of Eden to dress it and to keep it.* (To "keep" means to guard and protect.)
>
> Genesis 2:15

Now, I'm sure that you know what happened in the Garden of Eden. When Adam sinned, he lost his authority. But

Jesus restored that authority. Thank God we have it today. Thank God Satan is under our feet. Authority has been restored to you.

Seedtime and harvest did not come after the fall of man. Seedtime and harvest came at the creation of man. Some people think that seedtime and harvest is part of the curse. It's not; it's God's way of providing for you. If you don't have another thing in your life, please know that you've got authority, and you've got seed. You can come out of any situation when you have authority and seed, hallelujah. You can't stay in debt when you've got seed. You can't be limited when you've got seed. Your income can't be restricted when you've got seed. You, and only you, determine your destiny in life based upon the seeds that you sow. Don't let anything stop you from sowing your seed. Your life depends on it.

Chapter 3

CHAPTER 3
Learning To Protect Your Seed

Look Out for the Birds of Prey

We see Abram involved in offering a sacrifice to God, and notice what happens.

And he said, Lord God, whereby shall I know that I shall inherit it?

And he said unto him, Take me an heifer of three years old, and a she goat of three years old, and a ram of three years old, and a turtledove, and a young pigeon.

And he took unto him all these, and divided them in the midst, and laid each piece one against another: but the birds divided he not.

And when the fowls came down upon the carcases, Abram drove them away.

Genesis 15:8-11

In the Amplified it says, *And when the birds of prey* ***swooped down*** *upon the carcasses, Abram drove them away.*

Notice that before Abram could get his offering presented to God, *the birds of prey swooped down* and attempted to consume it.

That's exactly how our adversary, Satan, operates. This is a type and shadow of his devices. If there's any one thing Satan hates to see leave you and get to God, it's an offering. The reason is because that offering links you to the supernatural. Once an offering leaves your hands and is presented to God, then you are no longer limited to the world's way of producing increase. You are in covenant with the Almighty God.

From this story we see Abram preparing this sacrifice. He's busy. He's got blood all over him. He's working diligently. Every time he slices an animal the way God told him, he then lays it on the altar and turns around to cut another slice. But he notices that the birds of prey swoop down and attempt to devour his offering before he can present it to God.

The Bible says, *Abram drove them away.* Now when I read that phrase "drove them away," I do not picture Abram saying, "Get, birds." "Please stop." "Don't you understand, we're trying to do something spiritual?" It says *he drove them away.* I don't know how he did it. Perhaps he swatted them with his hand. Perhaps he picked up a stick of some sort. We do know that he used force! You don't use the term "drove them away" if there's not force behind it. Had he not driven them away, then they would have persisted, and they would have totally consumed his offering.

Why was it important that he drive the birds of prey away? If he doesn't, they're going to consume his sacrifice. He had to stand guard over that sacrifice. He had to protect that sacrifice. And then when an enemy came in to try to steal it before he could present it to God, he had to use force and drive them away.

Now that didn't mean they left and never came back. Every time he turned around they were back. The devil's persistent. You can drive him away but the Bible says, "Stay alert. Be on guard." Why? Because that adversary of yours, the devil, is looking for an opportunity to devour.

To *devour* means "to consume completely." Those birds of prey did not intend to just peck around in that meat. They intended to consume it completely. They didn't intend to just taste it and then fly away. No, birds of prey intend to consume completely.

Satan: The Seed Eater

The word *swoop* from the Amplified means: "to snatch or to seize suddenly." The word *suddenly* gives the implication of "catching one off guard." That's the way these birds of prey operate. They snatch or seize away suddenly hoping to catch you off guard.

Now let's look at something Jesus taught His disciples in Mark chapter 4. Mark 4:3-4 says,

> *Hearken; Behold, there went out a sower to sow:*
>
> *And it came to pass, as he sowed, some fell by the way side, and the fowls of the air came and devoured it up.*

Now notice every time we see these birds of prey or these fowls of the air, they're always endeavoring to consume something. In verse 14 Jesus begins His explanation of this parable.

> *The sower soweth the word.*
>
> *And these are they by the way side, where the word is sown; but when they have heard,* ***Satan cometh immediately, and taketh away the word*** *that was sown in their hearts*
>
> Mark 4:14-15

In comparison of these two verses, we see the analogy that the fowls of the air represent Satan.

So what Abram was actually dealing with back there is not just birds, but Satan. Satan is attempting to keep that sacrifice from getting to God. Why? Because he knows if Abram's sacrifice ever gets to God, then Abram is no longer limited to natural means, natural wisdom, or natural ability. Now he's linked to the supernatural God. El Shaddai is on his side, and no weapon formed against him will prosper!

I'm going to give you a very simple definition of the word *devourer*. It literally means - "seed-eater."

Satan is the "seed-eater" and he's after your seed. The moment you receive your paycheck, you can count on it, he will show up. The moment you get your paycheck he'll say, "You can't afford to tithe this week. Don't you dare give God 10 percent. If you give God 10 percent, you won't be able to pay the light bill, you won't be able to pay the car note, you won't be able to buy any groceries." The birds of prey have swooped down, and they are after your seed.

Don't Eat Your Seed

Remember in Genesis 1 it says,

> *I have given you every herb bearing seed* (seeding seed).
>
> Genesis 1:29

What is *seeding seed?* That's the most important seed the farmer possesses. This seed is not for eating. This is not seed which you consume on yourself. This is seed for next year's harvest. You never consume the seeding seed. Seeding seed is for planting.

The next time the thought comes up in your mind, "I can't afford to sow," that was a bird of prey. That was Satan himself trying to consume your seed. He is the seed-eater. That's what he's after. Why? Because if your seed gets into God's hands, then there's no devil in hell that can stop you from being blessed, successful and prosperous.

I personally believe that your tithe (10 percent of your income) is your "seeding seed." Make sure you give it to God and never consume it on yourself. When you give it to God, then He will rebuke the "seed-eater" in your behalf.

Chapter 4

CHAPTER 4

The Law Of Sowing and Reaping

Whether you believe it or not, you are where you are today because of the seeds you've sown. The Bible is very clear about this, and you can read it for yourself in Galatians. Galatians 6:7 says, *For whatsoever a man soweth, that shall he also reap.*

I like what Charles Capps says, "If you're down to your last one dollar, don't dare spend it. Sow it. Don't eat your seed." Seed is for sowing.

You will never enter into the fullness of God's plan for your prosperity if God comes last. He wants the firstfruit.

The seed-eater wants to devour your substance. He wants to consume it completely. He hopes that he can persuade you to spend everything you've got so there's nothing left to sow. If anybody knows the laws of sowing and reaping, it's Satan. He knows the laws of sowing and reaping, and he doesn't want them working in your life.

That's why he's after your seed. Your seed affects your destiny. Your seed affects your future. What you sow today has everything to do with how you'll live tomorrow.

As long as I've got seed, then I'm in control of my financial destiny. I'm in control of my income. Satan can't stop me from being blessed when I'm applying God's law of sowing and reaping.

The more I sow, the greater my harvest. The greater my harvest, then the more I'm able to sow. So, what are you waiting for? Start sowing every time you see an opportunity, and watch how God will bring you into a life of abounding blessings.

Chapter
5

CHAPTER 5
Give Your Best

When I went to work for Kenneth Copeland back in 1971, I only had one suit. A lady who lived next door to us went to a rummage sale and bought me a suit for $15. I came to work for Brother Copeland in the middle of the summer with that one suit and it was 100 percent wool. I sweated like a hog all summer in that one suit. I wore it to every meeting. I believed God for ties so I could have a different look. Then one day I got another pair of slacks that I could wear with the suit coat, and I got a different look. I made 15 changes out of that one suit. One day, I said, "God, I'm in the ministry. I'm going to be a preacher. I need suits."

Brother Copeland and I went to Odessa, Texas, for a meeting. When Brother Copeland finished preaching, he had me so fired up I couldn't wait for the next meeting, so I went to the streets and started preaching in the streets everything I heard him preach in the meeting. One day, I went out into the streets in Odessa, and I found a young Mexican boy. He couldn't have been over 14 years old. I started preaching to him. He couldn't understand a word I said because he couldn't speak any English. Somehow I was able to convince him that I wanted to give him my only suit. He was less fortunate than I was. His clothes were rags. I said, "God, I'm going to sow this suit into this young boy's life." I gave him my only suit. It was the best that I had.

Later, I noticed a men's department store on Main Street in Odessa. It had a big sign in the window that read: "Men's suits half price." It wouldn't have made any difference if they were $1.50, I couldn't have bought one. I stood there and looked at that sign and thought, "O God, they're half price." I felt really strong about going in there and looking at them even though I didn't have a dime.

I walked in the store, and the gentleman asked me if he could help me. I said,

"I'm just looking." I asked, "Where are your suits for half price?"

He showed me all these suits. He said, "What size do you wear?"

I told him my size, and he put this suit on me that fit me perfect! Oh, it looked good on me. He put another one on. It looked good too!

He said, "You want me to write it up?"

I said, "No, no. I can't buy anything today." I started to walk out and the Spirit of God spoke to me and He said, "Tell him to hold them for you." I turned around and I said, "Sir, would you hold those suits for me?"

He said, "Why?"

I said, "Well, I just believe somehow, some way, God's going to give me the money before I leave this town, and I'm going to buy those suits. Would you hold them for me for 24 hours?"

He said, "I will."

I went back to my hotel. I walked up and down that floor. I prayed in the spirit, and I did everything I knew to do. Suddenly, there was a knock on the door. I opened the door, and it was A.W. Copeland, Brother Copeland's father. He said, "Jerry, where have you been?"

I said, "I've been out in the street preaching."

He said, "I've been looking for you all morning."

I said, "Why?"

He said, "Well, last night in the offering somebody gave me an envelope and told me to give it to you. In fact, on the front of this envelope it said 'Give this to the little boy that works for Brother Copeland.'"

I said, "What is it, Granddad?"

He said, "I don't know. It just says give it to you." I opened it, and it was the exact amount of money that those suits were going to cost at that store.

I ran over to the store, and when I walked in, I couldn't even talk in English. I walked in speaking in tongues.

He said, "What happened to you?"

I said, "I told you that God was going to give me the money." I said, "The money was waiting for me, and I didn't even know it." I said, "Sir, we've got a meeting tonight. Can you alter my suits? I've got to wear one of these tonight."

Then I took my money out of the envelope, and I laid it up on the counter. He took half of it, and he gave me the other half back. I said, "No sir, there's exactly the amount you quoted me in this envelope. Here."

He said, "Since you left, those suits went down from half to another half." He said, "Those suits are now half of half price." He said, "Now son, it's cold out there." He said, "Do you have a top coat?" I didn't even know what a top coat was. He said, "Well you know what, I just happen to have a winter coat that costs exactly what you've got left." That man blessed me.

From that moment, I have never been able to wear all the suits God has given me. I've had people chase me down to give me a suit. I've had people buy me suits everywhere I go.

I learned that I may not always have what I need, but I am never without the **seed** that will produce it.

Proverbs 11:24 says,

> *There is he that scattereth, and yet increaseth.*

One translation says, "It is possible to give it all away and yet become richer."

> *Honour the Lord with thy substance, and with the firstfruits of all thine increase.*
>
> Proverbs 3:9

Honor the Lord with **your substance and your tithe.** Don't stop with the tithe. Honor God with your own personal belongings. Why? God wants you to be a seed sower so that He can multiply your resources for sowing.

Malachi 3:10 says,

> *Bring ye all the tithes into the storehouse, that there may be meat in mine house, and prove me now herewith, saith the Lord of hosts, if I will not open you the windows of heaven, and pour you out a blessing, that there shall not be room enough to receive it.*

What's the promise to the person who obeys this command? "And I," God says, "I, personally will rebuke the seed-eater for your sake."

I looked in *Webster's Dictionary* for the definition of the word *rebuke,* and it means: to address in a sharp and severe disapproval; to reprimand, to force back and to command to stop. The reason you need to be a tither is so God can get involved with you in driving the seed-eater away with force. When you honor God with the firstfruits of your increase, then God personally gets involved in driving the seed-eater away. He says, "Stop it! That's enough!"

You will find that when you drive the seed-eater away and you bring your tithe to God, you can live far greater on the 90 percent that's left than you could on the 100 percent. That 90 percent will stretch far, far greater than the 100 percent you keep.

Just like Abram, the birds of prey are swooping down attempting to consume your seed, and it's time to drive them away. Use some force. Don't allow Satan to consume your seed. Make God's offering the number one priority in your life and everything else second. Now watch how God will bless you like never before.

For Those Who Don't Know Jesus, Would You Like To Know Him?

If you were to die today, are you certain that you would go to Heaven? If you have accepted Jesus Christ as your personal Lord and Savior, you can be assured that when you die, you will go directly into the presence of God in Heaven. If you have not accepted Jesus as your personal Lord and Savior, is there any reason why you can't make Jesus the Lord of your life right now? Please pray this prayer out loud, and as you do, pray with a sincere and trusting heart, and you will be born again.

Dear God in Heaven,

I come to You in the Name of Jesus to receive salvation and eternal life. I believe that Jesus is Your Son. I believe that He died on the cross for my sins, and that You raised Him from the dead. I receive Jesus now into my heart and make Him the Lord of my life. Jesus, come into my heart. I welcome You as my Lord and Savior. Father, I believe Your Word that says I am now saved. I confess with my mouth that I am saved and born again. I am now a child of God.

Dr. Jerry Savelle is a noted author, evangelist, and teacher who travels extensively throughout the United States, Canada, and around the globe. He is president of Jerry Savelle Ministries International, a ministry of many outreaches devoted to meeting the needs of believers all over the world.

Well-known for his balanced Biblical teaching, Dr. Savelle has conducted seminars, crusades and conventions for over twenty-five years as well as ministering in thousands of churches and fellowships. He is in great demand today because of his inspiring message of victory and faith and his vivid, and often humorous, illustrations from the Bible. He teaches the uncompromised Word of God with a power and an authority that is exciting, but with a love that delivers the message directly to the spirit man.

In addition to his international headquarters in Crowley, Texas, Dr. Savelle is also founder of JSMI-Kenya; JSMI-United Kingdom; JSMI-South Africa; JSMI Tanzania; and JSMI-Australia. In 1994, he established the JSMI Bible Institute and School of World Evangelism. It is a two-year school for the preparation of ministers to take the Gospel of Jesus Christ to the nations of the world.

The missions outreach of his ministry extends to over 50 countries around the world. JSMI further ministers the Word of God through its prison ministry outreach.

Dr. Savelle has authored many books and has an extensive video and cassette teaching tape ministry and a world-wide television broadcast. Thousands of books, tapes, and videos are distributed around the world each year through Jerry Savelle Ministries International.

Other Books by Jerry Savelle

From Devastation To Restoration

Walking In Divine Favor

Turning Your Dreams Into Reality

Turning Your Adversity Into Victory

Honoring Your Heritage Of Faith

Don't Let Go Of Your Dreams

Faith Building Daily Devotionals

The Force of Joy

If Satan Can't Steal Your Joy, He Can't Keep Your Goods

A Right Mental Attitude

The Nature Of Faith

The Established Heart

Sharing Jesus Effectively

How To Overcome Financial Famine

You're Somebody Special To God

Leaving The Tears Behind

For a complete list of tapes, books, and videos by Jerry Savelle, write or call:

Jerry Savelle Ministries International
P.O. Box 748
Crowley, Texas 76036
(817) 297-3155

Notes:

Notes: